Seriously Sick Bible Stuff

Seriously Sick Bible Stuff

by Ed Strauss
art by Erwin Haya

ZONDERVAN.com/
AUTHORTRACKER
follow your favorite authors

Seriously Sick Bible Stuff

Copyright © 2007 by Edward Strauss
Illustrations © 2007 by Erwin Haya

Requests for information should be addressed to:
Grand Rapids, Michigan 49530

Library of Congress Cataloging-in-Publication Data

Strauss, Ed, 1953-
 Seriously sick Bible stuff / written by Ed Strauss.
  p. cm. -- (2:52)
  ISBN-13: 978-0-310-71310-4 (softcover)
  ISBN-10: 0-310-71310-2 (softcover)
  1. Bible--Miscellanea--Juvenile literature. I. Title.
  BS539.S77 2007
  220.9'5--dc22   2006032490

Editor: Barbara Scott
Art direction & design: Merit Alderink

Printed in United States of America

07 08 09 10 • 5 4 3 2 1

CONTENTS

Introduction

Ever heard someone say, "I wish I could've lived during Bible times"? Or maybe your kid sister sighs, "If only I could've followed Jesus around." Chances are she's read too many picture books showing Jesus and his disciples in clean robes with shampooed hair strolling through sunny orchards. Butterflies flutter by and happy children skip through fields of flowers. No one is stepping in donkey dung.

Riiight. But when night hits, and your sister learns that "the Son of Man has no place to lay his head" (Matthew 8:20) — meaning everybody's *sleeping* in the orchard — she'll jump in her time machine and zap back to the twenty-first century. Most girls couldn't hack ancient Israel even if they had a *house* to sleep in. Don't laugh. Most boys couldn't either.

Life during Bible times was like growing up in a Third World country. A lot of boys today are spoiled. You're used to fresh food in the fridge, your own bedroom, hours of playtime every day, showers (when you clue in that you're dirty), and clean toilets to sit on. Take away your tacos, toys, TVs, and toilets, plunge into Bible days, and you'd go into shock.

Oh sure, large Roman cities had theaters, clean water, and sewage systems. Yeah, yeah, and the rich had fine clothes, feasts, and read poetry while slaves manicured their toenails. *But!* We're not talking about Roman cities here. We're talking about Israel, where most Jews lived in dusty villages and crowded towns and no one was manicuring their toenails. Toilets? They squatted over stinking, fly-infested holes in the yard.

For over a thousand years, from the time of Joshua till the time of Jesus, things barely changed in the land of Israel. These days somebody's always inventing something new. Back then there was hardly any new technology. There were no flat-screen TVs, no computer games, and no DVDs. There were no skateboards or bicycles. After a day's work, the Israelites sat around telling stories and playing games like checkers. And, well . . . that was *about it*.

Changed your mind? Don't wanna visit ancient Israel? Sorry, it's too late. You've already started reading. Now all you can do is pack your bags and prepare for time travel. You're going to get a look at what life was *really* like during Bible times. Don't forget the toilet paper. You'll *need* it. You won't see another roll for two—maybe three—thousand years.

Life in the Villages

Hillbilly Israelites

Israel was a skinny chunk of land along the Mediterranean Sea. Only problem was, most Israelites never saw the sea. For much of their early history, the Philistines controlled all the best beaches, so the Israelites stayed in little villages up in the hills and valleys. Civilized countries like Egypt thought that the Israelites were a bunch of hillbillies. That was not entirely true. Some Israelites lived in cities. But yeah, *most* of them were farmers.

The average village had about twenty houses with fifty adults and fifty kids. Do the math. That's five people per house, and the houses were *small* — about as big as a two-car garage. People didn't really *live* in houses though. Houses were just a safe place to sleep where the bears didn't bite. People spent most of their waking hours outdoors.

Speaking of outdoors, the Israelites planted wheat and barley in the valleys between the hills and grew grapes and olive trees and other stuff on the slopes. A village might have about forty oxen and three hundred sheep and goats. The oxen pulled plows, the sheep grew wool, and the goats gave milk. They used donkeys and oxcarts to carry stuff around.

Mud-Brick Houses

Most houses were made of dried mud bricks. The walls were so weak you could dig a hole through them with your hands — and some guys *did!* Rain wore holes in the walls too. The nasty news is that poisonous snakes sometimes lived in those holes. Yikes!

In Jesus' day, houses probably had only one or two rooms and almost zero privacy. Doorways were so narrow and low that adults had to bend down to en-

ter. Israelites didn't have too many windows either, so it was usually dark inside, except for the light of smoky oil lamps. The floor was made out of dirt — or clay if you could afford it.

Larger homes might have had four rooms. The open courtyard with a wall around it was "room" number one. Your mom ground grain, cooked, and wove cloth here, and everyone ate here. Your ox slept in room number two, the covered porch on the east wall. That's also where the plow and tools were stored. The family slept in room three on the west wall. Room four against the back wall was for food storage.

Simple, Bare Necessities

Okay, by now you've clued in that living in ancient Israel means things were basic. Well, *how* basic? Running water? Not a chance. Your mom or sister had to lug jugs of water from the village well. In wealthy homes you washed your feet before you trotted in the house, but only if the floor had tiles. In farmhouses, floors were just hard-packed dirt, so washing your feet was pointless.

Want a shower? Sure, stand in the courtyard and pour water on yourself. Yup, that will work.

Toilets? Oh right, *toilets*. Your bathroom was a stinking pit out in the courtyard. It buzzed so loud with flies it sounded like a beehive. You really had to keep the lid on that sucker.

11

FUN FACT:

Toilet paper didn't exist in ancient Israel. It didn't even exist in America until Joseph Gayetty invented it in 1857. Before then, people wiped with pages from mail order catalogs. Of course, they didn't have catalogs in ancient Israel, so, um, what did they use? Whatever they could find: their bare left hand, rags, wool, stones, and sticks. You name it. Most people preferred leaves. Some of the farm trees must've been almost leafless.

Oodles of Kids

Houses were small, but the more kids your mom had, the more blessed she felt she was. If she had ten boys running around, she thought that was just great. A guy named Heman had fourteen sons and three daughters (1 Chronicles 25:5). Some *he-man*, huh? You're wondering *why* so many kids, right? Just wait. We'll talk about chores soon enough.

Leaky Roofs

Roofs on the mud houses were flat. Branches or thorn bushes were laid on wood rafters, and clay was packed on top of that. These roofs were strong enough to walk on, but if you jumped on them, you'd knock holes in them. Can't you just hear Jewish moms telling their kids, "Joab! How many times must I *tell* you? Do *not* jump on the roof!"

Roofs weren't hard to tear apart either. Once Jesus was inside a crowded house, and four guys wanted him to heal their sick friend. When couldn't get to him, they ripped a big hole in the roof and lowered their buddy down to Jesus with ropes (Mark 2:1 – 4).

On hot summer nights the whole family slept up on the roof because the breeze made it cooler. People went up there to pray too. They even stored food there. Some rooftops were so cluttered with stuff that you could hide up there. Play hide-and-seek and you just *know* somebody's on the roof.

One problem was that when it rained during winter, the clay on the roof would wash away, and people in the house below got a shower! Leaky roofs had to be fixed all the time. And after all that rain, *grass* even grew on the rooftops!

Tunics and Cloaks

Jewish men wore a light robe called a tunic. It was made out of wool or linen and reached down to the ankles. When you were working — which was usually — you tucked it up into your belt. Some guys said, "Aw! Forget *this*!" and just wore short tunics all the time.

Men wore a cloak over the tunic. The cloak was made of thick wool, and it was like a blanket, so on hot days you slung it over your shoulder. When you sat down in the dirt, you folded it and used it as a rug. When you went to sleep, the dirty rug became your blanket.

When the prophet Elijah was caught up to heaven in a whirlwind, his cloak blew off — not surprising with all that wind. When it hit the ground, his buddy, Elisha, picked it up and wore it. He *needed* it! After all, he'd just finished tearing his own clothes apart (2 Kings 2:11 – 13).

Designer Duds and Underpants

Some people think that Jesus wore expensive designer clothes because his tunic was seamless, woven in one piece from top to bottom (John 19:23). Nuh-uh. Many tunics from Galilee were woven in one piece. It was standard issue. That was how they made tunics in Galilee.

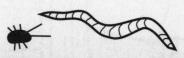

Jesus was no fashion show. After all, he was the one who said, "Do not worry . . . about your body, what you will wear" (Matthew 6:25). The rich Pharisees? Yeah, now *these* guys were the ones wearing fancy clothes.

By the way, the Bible calls Jesus' tunic his "undergarment." This is not talking about his underwear. People back then wore loincloths for underpants. *Undergarment* just means the tunic *under* his cloak. You know, like a T-shirt under a sweater.

Buying Stuff

Most boys get bored out of their skulls when Mom drags them to the mall to buy them clothes. Be thankful you didn't go out shopping in Bible times. Back then there were no price tags, so Mom might stand there arguing with a merchant over the price *for an hour*. They'd argue, haggle, and even yell at each other — and enjoy every minute of it! Ain't it great to live in the day of price tags?

Clean Clothes, Anyone?

Farmers weren't big on washing clothes because it was hard work to wash them by hand. Besides, it wore clothes out if you whacked them against the rocks *too* much. (Yep! That's how Moms washed clothes. *Smack! Whack! Splak!*) Anyway, the day after Mom washed your clothes, they started getting dirty again. And it's *not* like you had several sets of clothing. You wore the same tunic day after day and even slept in it.

Bedtime! What Fun!

There were no beds as we know them. You lay on a straw mat right on the dirt floor and covered yourself with your cloak. Most families slept on the floor together, so if you had to get up in the middle of the night for any reason, you ended up stepping on everyone else.

Israelites considered dogs so disgusting they wouldn't even *own* one, let alone keep one in the house. But farm animals? Sure. Every night Dad brought the milk goat into the house to sleep. (You're asking *why*, right? So no one stole it. Plus, the extra body heat kept the house warm.)

Apart from the smell, animals don't care where they poop. Goats will happily drop loads of dung balls just about anywhere. If you were an Israelite boy, guess whose job it would be to clean out the poop in the morning?

Just so this doesn't *totally* gross you out, the family slept on a floor eighteen inches higher than where the animals slept. This prevented poop balls from rolling across the floor to your sleeping mat. Makes a guy look forward to summer nights when you could sleep on the *roof*, huh?

Ash Heaps and Trash

Ovens were made of clay or stone and were usually outside in the courtyard. After all, your mom wouldn't want the house to smell like *smoke*, right? But when rainy season came, you had to cook indoors. Then things got smoky. Eventually the smoke escaped out a window.

Household trash? When the oven got full of ashes, Mom scraped them out and dumped them in a pile be-hind the house, along with broken pottery. When poor Job ended up covered with pus-filled boils, he went out behind his house, "took a piece of broken pottery and scraped himself with it as he sat among the ashes" (Job 2:8).

WHAT TO DO WITH THE DOO?

You have four guesses as to what happened to all the goat, donkey, sheep, and ox poo.

It was

(a) packed around the fruit trees

(b) dumped in a big ol' heap in the yard

(c) dried and used as fuel

(d) dumped into the toilet with the human excrement

If you guessed (a), you are *so* right! Jesus talked about a farmer fertilizing a fig tree. In the original Greek, *fertilize* means "to cast dung" (Luke 13:8). Wow! They *threw* the stuff? One of the biggest blessings farmers wanted was to sit peacefully under a fig tree and think (Micah 4:4). You'd wanna pick a tree that hadn't been dunged recently.

If you guessed (b), you are also right! Dung ended up in the dunghill. These days the polite term is *manure pile*. The Israelites sometimes beefed up their valuable fertilizer by trampling straw in it with their feet. In Isaiah 25:10–11, God says the Moabites would "spread out their *hands* in it, as a swimmer spreads out his hands to swim." Hey! Wanna be on the Moabite swim team in the Bronze Age Olympics?

If you guessed (c), the answer is *also correct*. When God told Ezekiel to burn human poop and Ezekiel got grossed out, God told him he could cook his food over flaming cow manure instead (Ezekiel 4:15).

The only wrong answer in this quiz was (d). Toss animal dung down the toilet with human waste. C'mon! That's wasteful!

Get Smarter

The Hebrew word *Madmenah* means "Dunghill," and it was similiar to the names of two Israelite towns named Madmannah (See Joshua 15:31 and Isaiah 10:31). Some Bible scholars say these were fertilizer-producing centers. You'd think that only a madman would live in Madmannah, but hey, they had loads of dung. Why throw the stuff away when you can sell it?

On the other hand, smart Israelites found work elsewhere. Only the most desperate people took such filthy jobs. The Bible says God lifts the needy "out of the dunghill" (Psalm 113:7, *KJV*). It was the kind of job you prayed God would get you *out* of.

Don't want to live in Manure Pile? Hey, like your parents say, if you want a *good* job when you grow up, study hard now. Sometimes school is boring, but it's even more boring to have a dead-end job and low wages for the rest of your life.

The Malls of Hazor

There were no shopping malls in Bible times, but there *were* shops. Every so often there was a city, and cities had market streets. Spend a day in town and, wow, you got to see shops of carpenters, mat weavers, potters, bakers, cheese makers, goldsmiths, or farmers selling vegetables. Exciting, huh?

Of course, cities back then were pretty small. Little ones covered only an acre or two and had a few hundred people. (That's a *city*? Yup.) A world-class city like Hazor spread over 175 acres and had a population of 40,000. Ho! *Monster* metropolis or what?

Back then, cities usually sat on a hill and had high stone walls. Being on a hill was a must. You never could tell when an enemy army might want to try attacking you. (Yeah, to rob your fancy "mall.")

Sometimes the markets had more than just cheese and bread. Sometimes there was stuff from other countries. Israel was on the caravan roads between Syria and Egypt, and camels constantly plodded through, loaded with spices and silk and perfume and all kinds of high-priced goodies.

When is Garbage Day?

There are, um, some things about ancient cities you should know. Like, they were usually crowded and had narrow streets and alleys zigzagging all over the place. Worse yet, there was no garbage collection. It was like a permanent New York City garbage strike. So where did rubbish end up? If it was small stuff, it got chucked into the alleys. Folks weren't particular back then and there weren't laws against littering. But if, say, your goat died, it's not like you could get away with dumping it in the street. You had to haul *that* away.

The Local Dump

Jerusalem had a huge, open, stinky garbage dump just outside the city in the Valley of Hinnom (Gehenna). All day and all night long, fires burned the garbage, popping and sizzling and sending up foul-smelling smoke. Usually the wind carried the smoke away, but sometimes it blew back toward the city.

The Gehenna Dump was just swarming with flies, and fly maggots squirmed in and out of rotting food and oozing dead things and dung. The Gehenna Dump was so bad that Jesus used it to describe what *hell* was like — a place where "their worm does not die, and the fire is not quenched" (Mark 9:47 – 48).

NOT-SO-FUN FACT:

Sometimes enemy armies surrounded ancient cities and besieged them for years, not letting anyone in or out. When the people inside the city ran out of food and water, they might be forced to eat their own dung and drink their own urine.
(See Isaiah 36:12.)

The Dung Gate

The dump was just outside the *Dung Gate*, and if that doesn't give you an idea of the kind of make-you-gag garbage that was dragged through it, nothing will. Rubbish, garbage, carcasses, dung, you name it.

You gotta wonder what Nehemiah was thinking when he sent the choir out singing. He said, "I also assigned two large choirs to give thanks. One was to proceed on top of the wall to the right, toward the Dung Gate" (Nehemiah 12:31). Well, they had just *rebuilt* the Dung Gate, so it didn't stink so badly yet. Otherwise the singers might've gagged and fallen off the wall.

Sewage in the City

You won't find it in the New International Version — the translators were too polite — but the King James Version of the Bible talks six times about men urinating against the city walls (1 Kings 14:10). You just *gotta* know that with thousands of men and boys watering the walls every day—get a few sunny days in a row and, *Whoooeeee!* — them walls would reek!

Back then, most Israelite cities had no sewage systems—just open gutters that ran along alleys. These yellow streams trickled down the streets. Israel was dry and dusty, so when Isaiah 10:6 talks about "mud in the streets," it's not necessarily talking about rain mixing with dust to make this (ahem) "mud."

And were you wondering where city folks did "number two"? They had toilets in their courtyards. If you wonder what on earth they did when their toilets got full, well, we won't even go there.

PUBLIC LATRINES

Derek Dundee of Mallabassa, Missouri asks: "Did Israelite men only pee on walls? That's gross!" No, Derek, if a building was torn down, guys would urinate among the rubble too. After King Jehu demolished the temple of Baal, the Israelites used it as a public latrine (urinal) for hundreds of years (2 Kings 10:27). Must've been real stinky by that time, 'cause, like, no one ever cleaned it!

Street Cleaners

There were no garbage men or street cleaners in ancient Israel — not *human* at least. But ever see a nature show where buzzards are gulping down a rotten corpse and the narrator says, "The vulture is the garbage collector of Africa"? And jackals are such good scavengers that they're called "street cleaners" in many African cities.

Back in Israel, the cleaning crews were canines. The

dogs of the day looked like dirty coyotes. They prowled around the cities, half wild, as they ate garbage. As far as the dogs were concerned, there wasn't *enough* garbage, and they often wandered around howling and looking for food. It's a good thing they *did* clean the streets! That's where little boys and girls played (Zechariah 8:5)!

GET STRONGER

Does your bedroom look like some alley in ancient Israel? If there are dirty duds ditched on the floor and discolored underpants decorating the doorknobs, you need to do some serious "street cleaning." (Don't count on any wild dogs doing the job for you.)

Worse yet, does your room look like the Jerusalem dump, with mold growing on plates of abandoned spaghetti under your bed, and maggots crawling through half-eaten peaches? Listen, an important part of being a man is keeping things neat. God told King Hezekiah that the most important job he had to do before he died was to put his house in order (2 Kings 20:1). So why not start with your heart and then tackle your room?

Staying Clean

Back two and three thousand years ago, the Jews had no idea that germs existed. Israel was a dirty, dusty country full of manure piles, flies, fleas, lice, and disease-carrying animals, so how did people survive? Fortunately for them, Moses' Law ordered them to "bathe with water" (Leviticus 15:11). Result: Jews washed their hands a lot, especially before eating food. God's people may have been clueless about germs, but God knew.

Just the same, germs multiplied like crazy all around them — in the dirt, in the dung, in the water — so people still got sick *all* the time.

Doctors & Medicine

Think you have it rough when you have to go to the doctor for a shot? The nurse says,

"This won't hurt," but you see the size of the needle and think of making a run for it? Is it a hassle to take pills three times a day to get rid of an ear infection? Listen, you never had it so good!

Back in Israel when folks got sick, they often *stayed* sick. There were only a few doctors, and they didn't know much. Luke, who probably wrote the gospel of Luke, was a doctor himself (Colossians 4:14). He did his best, but medicine was limited back then.

In fact, only one hundred years ago — almost two thousand years *after* Jesus — travelers to Israel reported that the land was overrun with sick people. Everywhere they looked, they saw people who were blind, sick, crippled, or leprous.

IN LINE FOR HEALING

To get an idea how many people were sick at one time, when Jesus was in Capernaum, people brought the sick to him. "The *whole town* gathered at the door, and Jesus healed *many* who had various diseases" (Mark 1:33–34). Problem was, before Jesus showed up, there were very few healers. Sure, Naaman got healed of leprosy, and King Hezekiah got cured of a killer boil, but these were exceptions. *Usually* if you had leprosy it ate you alive. Or if you got a killer boil, it killed you!

The Pox

Smallpox has plagued people for thousands of years. When you got the pox, your whole body was covered with pimples. They grew bigger, filled with pus, and then finally covered over with scabs. Some Bible experts say Job's boils were smallpox. Job complained, "My body is clothed with worms and scabs, my skin is broken and festering" (Job 7:5). Yeah, *worms*. Worms were crawling in and out of Job's pus-filled scabs. He looked so disgusting that people probably ran away when he came around.

NOT-SO-FUN FACT

Smallpox was once so common that it killed hundreds of millions of people and left others blind or covered with scars. It wasn't till 1796 that Dr. Jenner created a vaccine to stop smallpox. Still longing for the "good ol' days"?

Going Crazy Scratching

The Bible refers to "the itch, from which you cannot be cured" (Deuteronomy 28:27), and that sounds exactly like scabies. Back then people didn't know that an eensy creature called a mite digging under their skin caused scabies, and they had no idea how to cure it. What they *did* know was that they itched until it nearly drove them crazy. And it was contagious — meaning that everyone who came in contact with you got it too. People still get scabies today, but modern medicines zap it.

Fleas and Disease

Ever seen a photo of flea enlarged a thousand times? It looks like some alien monster, right? Well, considering they carry diseases like the bubonic plague and typhus, they *are* monsters! Seven hundred years ago, the bubonic plague killed 25,000,000 people in Europe alone!

Fleas hang out on rats, but when the plague killed the rats, the fleas hopped to humans. When the Philistines captured the ark of God from Israel, soon rats overran their cities — then plague broke out. The Philistines knew that God was judging them. They even figured out that the rats were somehow involved (1 Samuel 5; 6:1 – 5). They just didn't put their finger on the fleas.

Leprosy

Leprosy is a terrible disease. It causes lumps on your body that turn into open sores. These days there are medicines to fight it, but if you got leprosy in ancient Israel, you were forced to leave home and live away from other people. You wore torn clothes, kept your hair messy, and walked around shouting, "Unclean! Unclean!" to keep people away (Leviticus 13:45 – 46).

Some people think leprosy was no problem because Jesus could heal it. True, he could. But he didn't heal every leper. And what about the thousands of years before he was born? Jesus said, "There were *many* in Israel with leprosy in the time of Elisha the prophet, yet not one of them was cleansed — only Naaman the Syrian" (Luke 4:27).

Malaria

Back then, when a mosquito drilled you for blood and gave you malaria, you'd basically had it. There was no quinine, and when you don't treat malaria, it causes one high fever after another until you finally die. Many experts believe that the high fever that Peter's mother-in-law had was malaria. Good thing Jesus dropped by for lunch that day and cured her (Luke 4:38 – 39).

Puking your Guts up

Herod Agippa died because his guts got infested with intestinal roundworms, but he wasn't the only guy to get those suckers. *You* could've ended up with them too! They were common back then. They still do their dirty work in countries where people don't have clean water or good sewage systems.

These worms can grow sixteen inches long, and they're like humongo straws sucking up the juices inside your bowels. Sometimes they get all twisted together in a clump and block up your intestines. This causes major pain, and suddenly you're puking up worms, gagging, and puking some more (Acts 12:23).

Dysentery and Diarrhea

When poop gets into food, it causes a disease called dysentry. Now think about it: how does *that* happen? You guessed it! Usually someone goes number two and then doesn't wash his hands. The poop ends up in the food or the water, and soon your family has diarrhea, pain in their bowels, sores, and infections. There was a *lot* of dysentery in Bible days. Even the father of Publius, a rich Roman ruler, was sick in bed with it (Acts 28:8).

And There's More

You think this stuff was bad? What about festering boils, tuberculosis, gangrene, dropsy, and eye diseases? And hey, we haven't even mentioned hepatitis A, typhoid fever, cholera, etc. Well, I guess *now* we have.

GET COOLER

Modern scientists have conquered lots of diseases, but there are still tons of germs around that can kill you or leave you puking. And oodles of these diseases are contagious. It's bad enough if *you're* sick in bed with dysentery, or have your hair full of head lice, or you're scratching scabies—but for *sure* you don't want your friends and family to get what you have. Right?

If you don't want to spread diseases to others, stay clean. "Bathe with water" (Leviticus 15:11). Wash your body, wash your hair, and *especially* wash your hands with soap! Wash them after petting the dog, scrub them after going to the toilet (*puh-leeze!*), and clean them before eating. It beats walking around yelling, "Unclean! Unclean!"

39

The Local Water

The water in the local well was safe — *usually*. But get too much rain, and the germs in the piles of manure seep down into the water supply. Next thing you know the whole village has dysentery and diarrhea!

Often dust storms blew into town. To keep the dust out, many wells had big stone lids. But some wells had no lids, meaning that your ox could lean over to look and fall in headfirst. When that happened, Israelites immediately pulled him out (Luke 14:5). It wasn't just to save the ox. Often *el toro* didn't survive the dive. No, you had to get the body out before he lay there and rotted in your drinking water.

When droughts hit Israel, the wells ran dry, so almost every town had a cistern, a large underground tank. The cistern filled up during the rainy season, then stored the water for months — or years. But when water sits too long, it becomes stagnant and tastes stale. And drink it all the way down to the germ-filled mud on the bottom and you were sick for sure!

No Juice or Pop

If you were thirsty, there was no corner store where you could buy a "brain freeze." If you got tired of plain water, there was always lots of goat's milk — *warm* goat's milk (Proverbs 27:27). Or better yet, warm *sour* goat's milk, slowly turning itself into yogurt. Imagine coming home from school thirsty and your mom pours you a glass of that.

TWO SQUARE MEALS A DAY

There was no free lunch in ancient Israel. Well, actually, there was no breakfast. People ate only two meals: brunch and dinner. You chewed healthy food though, like roasted grain, bread, cheese, fish, raisins, dried figs, and nuts. That kind of natural food's good for you!

The downside was that you only got fruits or veggies that were in season. No one was trucking in melons from Florida in winter. You only ate pomegranates in pomegranate season and fresh figs in fig season. Even Jesus couldn't get figs out of season (Mark 11:12–13).

If you wanted Chinese food, you had to travel all the way to China.

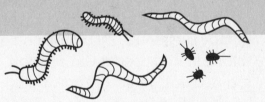

Bread

Bread was made out of wheat or barley and shaped like buns or pizza crusts — but without the salami or cheese or anchovies. Don't even *think* about pizza. Pizza hadn't been invented yet. People ate plain bread . Sometimes they dipped it in vinegar or oil. Yum!

FUN FACT

In ancient Israel, the baker kept a furnace going to bake bread. Good thing! Matches hadn't been invented yet, so when it was time to cook, Israelite moms probably sent their kids to the baker's shop with a piece of a broken pot. Kids would line up, and the baker would give each of them a burning coal in their broken bowl, and they'd run it home to Mom. Nowadays there'd be a dozen laws against that.

Finger Food

The Israelites didn't use forks or spoons. When a family ate, they all stuck their fingers in a big bowl and fished out what they wanted. If they were eating something gloopy like lentils, they broke off a piece of thin bread, folded it, and used it like a spoon. Okay, before you're grossed out, ya gotta know that they were big into washing their hands before meals.

Beans & Lentils

People ate beans and lentils almost every day, often in a stew with onions, garlic, and spices. This is what Esau traded his birthright for. Lentils and beans were even mixed with grain to make bread. Eating beans with garlic meant that "fluffing your robes" or "tootin' in your tunic" was a constant problem. That was tolerable if you were sleeping on the roof and the wind was blowing, but the smell could really gag you in a one-room house. Especially if you had a big family and you were *all* adding to the atmosphere.

SIT UP STRAIGHT?

The Israelites weren't really into chairs. Bowls of food were set on a rug on the floor—or out in the courtyard—and everyone knelt around it or sat with their legs folded. In Roman times, some Jews had tables. The wealthy families used benches but they didn't *sit* on them. On special occasions, such as Passover, they *reclined* on them—which means lying down, propped up on one elbow. The head of the guy next to you would be beside your chest, and your feet would be behind him. You were often *leaning* on someone while you ate.

Where's the Beef?

The kings of Israel were often big meat eaters, but meat was expensive, so the average Israelite hardly ever ate meat, except on special feasts or at Passover. When the Prodigal Son came home and his father roasted the fattened calf, the older brother complained that he had never even had a goat barbeque (Luke 15:29).

Chickens and Sparrows

In Jesus' day, Jews raised chickens. These days, moms and dads clean up especially well after cutting up raw chicken. Back then, moms and dads didn't know that you shouldn't chop veggies on the same board where you chopped up chicken—so the Israelites were probably puking sick with salmonella.

Most people with chickens couldn't afford to cook them, though, 'cause they needed the eggs. If they wanted fried fowl, it was usually sparrows. Five sparrows sold for two "pennies" (Luke 12:6). That sounds cheap, but workers earned so little that the poorest people could hardly even eat sparrows.

Tilapia & Other Fish

People who lived near the Sea of Galilee ate a lot of fish. Here's some *good* news: fish were healthier back then. These days, tilapia raised in some Third World countries are fed nothing but chicken poop. No joke. Back then, tilapia in the Sea of Galilee didn't have a crappy diet. In fact, they were so tasty that they were dried and salted and shipped all over the place — as far away as Rome. Mind you, there *were* bottom feeders that had to be chucked back in the water.

Garden Vegetables

When the Israelites lived in Egypt, they ate all kinds of vegetables. In fact, they enjoyed them *so much* that they almost called off their invasion of the Promised Land to go back for another helping—even if it meant becoming slaves again! They wailed, "We remember the fish we ate in Egypt . . . also the cucumbers, melons, leeks, onions and garlic" (Numbers 11:5). You gotta *wonder* about people who were willing to become slaves again just to eat onions and garlic, but there's no accounting for taste.

Garlic Galore

Garlic has a *very* strong taste. Eat enough of it and you get garlic sweat and killer breath. Garlic is only mentioned *once* in the Bible (Numbers 11:5), and some people figure that's enough. But hey, it's a natural medicine and helped keep the Jews healthy. It was the one spice that germs were afraid of. Eat enough garlic and the mosquitos won't even bite you.

SPICING UP THE FOOD

King Solomon loved spiced-up food! He had a huge garden where he grew spices like calamus, cinnamon, aloes, and incense trees. A thousand years later, ordinary Jews still grew spices in their gardens, especially stuff like mint, dill, and cummin.

Why spice, you ask? Well, it wasn't just for the taste! Back then there were no fridges. Bread left out too long would get covered with mold. Or flies would lay eggs on the goat cheese, and a few days later maggots were tunneling through it, pooping as they went. Back then, cooks used spices to cover food that had gone "off" and tasted bad—meaning that if the lentil stew was left out all day and was swarming with germs, Mom just added spice so you couldn't tell the difference. But spices didn't kill germs. They just come out tasting like mint.

Desserts and Treats

Yes, there were desserts in Israel. There was no sugar, but there was honey, as well as sweet syrup made from boiling dates. Pastries were covered with honey and fruit, and candies were made of dates, honey, almonds,

and pistachios. In fact, Israel had so *much* honey and sweets that they exported tons of it to cities like Tyre (Ezekiel 27:17).

Boiling dates was not a problem, but getting honey could be tricky. Wild bees are fierce, and honey collectors often ended up running and howling with swarms of bees chasing them.

Pistachios, almonds, walnuts, and figs grew all over Israel. Figs were dried and pressed into flat cakes. You still see them sold in stores that way today. Grapes were also dried and pressed into raisin cakes. One day King David felt real generous and gave every man and woman in Jerusalem a cake of dates and a cake of raisins. Yeah, that's right. The *adults* got the goodies. The kids *didn't*. Hey, David knew the parents would share (1 Chronicles 16:3).

Poor People's Food

Well-to-do Israelites ate wheat bread, but the poor mostly ate cheaper barley bread. Can't even afford barely bread? Eat figs. They were so plentiful that they were called "the poor man's food." Some people were *so* poor they didn't even have money to buy figs. What did they eat?

They ate the roots of the broom tree. Yikes! Those suckers are poisonous! (By the way, it's *not* called a broom tree because its wood was used to make brooms.) The exiles also ate mallows (not *marsh*mallows). Mallows are called *salt plants* and grow in the desert. They have about as much nutritional value as cardboard (Job 30:4).

GET DEEPER

Before eating a meal, Jesus always thanked God for the food they were about to eat. Many Christian families still say grace to this day. It's important to be grateful, even when you're not crazy about the taste of some of the food. Be thankful that you *have* good, nutritious food. Millions of kids in poor countries are hungry all the time. In fact, right now, and every single day, *thousands* of children die from lack of food.

We have so much to be thankful for. We have nice homes, good food, comforts, and all kinds of stuff that we don't really need. Next time you're tempted to grumble and complain, remember how much you have to be thankful for.

Toys & Playtime

There were toys in ancient Israel, but by the time you were a tween, you didn't spend the whole day goofing off and playing like many kids do today. Besides, their toys were like baby's rattles and little clay horses. You *really* wanna play with that stuff? Okay, okay. They also had marbles and balls. Not basketballs, but probably balls made out of leather and filled with straw. When they weren't busy working, kids played in the city streets, racing, wrestling, playing tag, or kicking the ball around.

Family Time and Games

There were no video games, movies, or skateboards, but at the end of the day, families sat around and told stories. Sometimes the whole village hung out and played music, sang, and danced. (These were folk dances, by the way, sort of like religious line dancing.)

Parents and kids also played games like checkers and backgammon. Yup! They had board games, and Jesus probably played them too. Games were so popular that game boards and markers have been dug up in almost every single archaeological site in Israel. Probably the big event in the village was watching old Baruch and Zeke battle it out on the checkers board.

"LET'S PLAY FUNERAL"

Kids back then didn't play cops and robbers, but they *did* do some pretty weird playacting. Sometimes the girls would say, "Let's have a wedding parade!" They'd play a flute and try to get the boys to join them singing and dancing around. *Not!*

Boys would rather play dead man. Some kid would lie stiff and pretend to be the corpse, and other boys would carry him down the street on a mat. They'd sing a dirge (funeral song) and try to get the girls to be mourners, crying and wailing. "*Yeah. Like that* really sounds like fun," girls complained. (See Luke 7:32.)

School Time

There were no public schools in Israel in Old Testament days. Priests and wealthy people could read and write, but most ordinary folk never went to school. So what did kids learn? They learned practical stuff while working, plus parents told them Bible stories and the laws of Moses.

Need a letter written? You had to pay a scribe to write it. You could always pick out a scribe in the crowd. He was the guy carrying a writing kit and paper and ink around with him.

You'll be happy to know that by Jesus' day there were schools. Only boys were educated, though. That's right—girls didn't have to go. Actually, they didn't *get* to go. From age five, boys spent half a day in the synagogue where they learned the alphabet and read from the Bible. By noon, school ended and then they went home and worked.

All in a Day's Work

Farmers' kids helped on the farm at an early age. Girls helped their moms weave cloth, grind grain, cook, weed the garden, milk the goat, and lug jugs of water from the well. Boys helped their dads plow and plant and harvest. They scooped up dung, dug rocks out of the soil, and pruned grapevines. Sometimes you sat in your courtyard helping your dad mend and sharpen farm tools. And boys did a lot of other stuff too.

Pokey Firewood

Gathering firewood for your cooking fire was no fun. Israel was not like Maine with a zillion square miles of forests. In Israel, all they had were scrubby little bushes and thorn bushes. Solomon talked about the *snap crackle pop* of thorns burning under a pot, and David talked about cooking pots "feeling" the thorns (Ecclesiastes 7:6; Psalm 58:9). Well, the *pots* may not have felt the thorns, but *you* sure would as you gathered them! People tried all kinds of ways to gather thorns without getting hurt. You can see why some folks gave up and burned cow dung instead. Hey, want to gather *that*?

Sitting and Staring

Kids had some *very* boring jobs. One was shepherd-
ing. If your family owned sheep, you might have had to
sit on the hillside, bored out of your skull, watching the
sheep graze. A guy named Jacob complained about
how tough a shepherd's life was. He said, "The heat
consumed me in the daytime and the cold at night, and
sleep fled from my eyes" (Genesis 31:40). Of course,
if bears or lions or wolves attacked, things could get
exciting really fast. Then it could be more than the *heat*
consuming you.

Grape-herding

Another boring job was guarding the vineyard every
May and June when the grapes began to ripen. The
vineyards were on the hillsides, and your dad would
build a little shelter under the grapevines, and there
you sat — and sat and sat and sat — day and night for
two months, grape-herding. If your sister remembered,
she would bring you meals.

Hey, *someone* had to keep thieves from grabbing your
grapes. Someone had to check the leaves and grapes
for worms. Someone had to throw rocks at the hungry
foxes. Someone had to be there when a savage, wild
boar with curved, deadly, death-dealing tusks and
bone-crunching teeth broke in.

Defending the Cukes

The Israelites loved cucumbers. On a dusty day, a delicious, juicy cuke was an ideal snack. But critters called slugs also loved cucumbers. These slimy slugs slipped into your garden at night and ate the tender leaves. Guess whose job it would've been to stay up late and slug it out with the slugs? *Yours*, buddy!

Melancholy over Melons

Back in Egypt, people grew watermelons, as well as muskmelons like cantaloupes and honeydews. After the Israelites split Egypt and were staggering across the desert, they spent a *lot* of time thinking about the big, red, juicy watermelons along the Nile. So what did they plant as soon as they took over Canaan? Melons!

When melons were small and unripe, Israelites put up scarecrows to keep birds away. God compared these brainless straw men to idols. Jeremiah 10:5 says, "Like a scarecrow in a melon patch, their idols cannot speak." Can you picture pagans bowing down to a scarecrow? No. But they prayed to idols.

If your family owned a big melon patch, when the melons were ripe, you had to sit in a little hut there for a month guarding them. What on earth does a person *think* about day after day, mulling among the melons?

INCOMING LOCUST STORM!

Sometimes droughts and locusts wiped out your hard work. A drought was bad enough, because all year you had to lug jugs of water from the well to your dry orchard. But sometimes humongo clouds of locusts swept in and devoured everything in sight.

One year the Israelites drifted away from God, so he sent a drought complete with *four waves* of locusts! The grain fields vanished, the grapevines were gobbled—leaves and all. The bark was even ripped off fig trees (Joel 1:4–7). It was like a tornado with teeth!

Plodding Behind the Plow

Other months, like during plowing season, you worked from sunrise to sundown. Plowing behind a team of oxen was tiring work. Not only did you need to keep poking the oxen in the butt with a goad (a sharp, iron-tipped rod) to make them move, but the plows were practically useless. If the field was stony or had lots of weeds, you had to plow it over and over again.

After a few days of that, you'd probably feel like doing what Elisha did — he killed the oxen and burned the plow. (Okay, okay, *just kidding*.) Elisha was sacrificing his oxen to God. Read the story in 1 Kings 19:19 – 21.

Ox goads kept wearing out and had to be "repointed." While they never seemed sharp enough to be able to make the oxen move fast, a farmer named Shamgar found that they made dandy weapons. He used his goad to take out six hundred Philistines (Judges 3:31).

Rain and Wind

Israel had two short rainy seasons a year — one in September and one in December. Well, you might have gotten a bit more rain in spring, but that was *it*. Then summer hit — six months of heat and dust. Sometimes a scorching wind whistled in from the desert, blowing sand and dust in your eyes. If only a little rain fell, things got really dry. If *no* rain fell, then the whole year was just one long hot, dusty, thirsty summer. And *this* before the invention of slushies!

Harvest Season

Two other times you worked your buns off were barley harvest and wheat harvest — from April to June. This was backbreaking work, 'cause wheat and barley only grew a couple feet high. So you had to bend over all day long, grab one handful at a time, and cut it with a small hand sickle. Women came along behind you, tied the stalks of grain into bundles, and stood them up to dry.

This was in the heat of summer, so you had to watch that you didn't get too much sun. Sunstroke could make you sick as a dog or even kill you. You stopped in the middle of the day to eat and rest in a little shelter, and then — just when you got comfortable — you were back up and at it.

Heat Waves

Speaking of the sun, temperatures in the summertime
were sizzling by noon, turning the whole country into
an oven. And there was no air conditioning! When it
got hot, you basically crawled into the shade and sat
it out. That's why farmers practically *lived* under the
shade of vineyards or fig trees or olive trees. King Saul
camped out under a pomegranate tree — not so smart,
since those dinky little trees give almost *zero* shade.
But then, Saul wasn't exactly the brightest king Israel
ever had (1 Samuel 14:2).

Threshing and Winnowing

Carting: When the grain was all cut, the bundles were loaded onto an oxcart and taken to the threshing area. Loaded carts were heavy. One day God warned some evil Israelites, "I will crush you as a cart crushes when loaded with grain" (Amos 2:13). Best not to fall asleep in the road when God's rolling by.

Threshing: At the threshing area, the bundles of grain were spread on the ground, and a couple oxen walked in circles, trampling them to break the papery husks off the grain. They loved this job 'cause they got to eat grain as they went in circles. You'd want to be sure the oxen had *already* pooped before they did the grain walk thing.

The oxen dragged a heavy wooden sled over the grain to separate it from the husks. Maybe the kids got to ride on the sled to add extra weight to it. Fun!

Winnowing: Once the grain was threshed, you winnowed it. You used shovels to flip the grain into the air so the wind could carry the husks away. Winnowing was fun at first, but after a while you got dust all over you and prickly husks inside your clothing.

Sifting: When only grain was left, your sister had to sit there for days, sifting the grain through a sieve to get out the pebbles. You hoped she did a good job, otherwise you'd chip your teeth on rocks when eating bread. She also had to sift out the seeds of tares (weeds) 'cause if your mom baked those in your bread, you'd be vomiting.

Blood of Grapes!

Moses talked about Israelites drinking "the foaming blood of the grape" (Deuteronomy 32:14). Whoa! What were these people *drinking*? Was this Klingon blood wine? Were these the grapes of wrath? No, just regular wine.

You see, after the wheat harvest, the Israelites began harvesting grapes. Some of the grapes were gobbled right away, others were set out in the sun to shrivel up into raisins, but most were dumped into huge stone pits where men and women stomped them.

It was like a food fight. Your skin ended up red, your hair was red, and your clothes were red. The Bible talks about a guy called Judah "washing" his robes in the blood of grapes (Genesis 49:11), and this was *it*, buddy! Your mom could bleach your clothes for a week and not get the stains out!

NOT-SO-FUN FACT

If you were an Israelite slave working for an Israelite master, he wasn't supposed to treat you badly. Of course, he might still beat you. The bad news is, he might blind one of your eyes or bash out one of your teeth. The good news is, if he did that he had to let you go free (Exodus 21:26 – 27).

It's Raining Olives!

Harvesting olives was fun for kids 'cause you got to whack the branches with sticks, and hundreds of olives rained down on you. There were tons of olive trees in Israel, and each tree produced enough olives to make twenty gallons of oil. And talk about a lot of oil: King Solomon gave King Hiram "twenty thousand baths of pressed olive oil" (1 Kings 5:11). This doesn't mean Hiram bathed in olive oil. That woulda been weird. Twenty thousand *baths* is another way of saying 115,000 *gallons*.

Daze of Rest

By the time Sabbaths and Feast days rolled around, you were good and ready for them. When you finished a week of work, you were dazed and ready to doze. Today lots of people think it's odd that the Jews did nothing but rest every Saturday. "Worship God? Right! But I can't do *any*thing else?" Listen, back then when Sabbath rolled around, you were ready to rest.

Poorest of the Poor

Some people were so poor that they didn't own any land. They worked as hired hands on other people's land. If nobody was hiring, well, they just stood in the marketplace doing nothing and getting hungry. Sometimes they got upset and started riots.

Sold into Slavery

In ancient Israel, when people got so poor that they couldn't pay their debts or taxes, they sometimes sold their daughters and sons into slavery (Nehemiah 5:4–5). Hey, it's not like dads back then *wanted* to do that, but sometimes they were forced to.

Slavery was not fun. For starters, you were dragged away from your family and friends. Not many slaves ended up like Daniel and pals — given royal food and sent to school in Babylon. Usually when you became a slave, you had to work from sunrise to sunset until you felt brain-dead.

Get Stronger

Most kids wouldn't mind riding on an ox sled. That kind of work is fun. But what *really* counts is if you help around the house when the work is not so fun. Do you do your part and help out, or are you just there for the ride?

Jesus told a story about a farmer who had two sons. The farmer asked the first son to go work in the vineyard. The son promised *sure, sure,* he'd do it, but he didn't get off his butt and actually *go* to the vineyard. It's not like he forgot. He probably said he'd do it just to get his dad off his back. If his brother hadn't picked up the slack, the job wouldn't have gotten done (Matthew 21:28–31).

The moral of this story is simple: If you *say* you'll do your chores, *do* them.

Learning a Trade

When I Grow Up

Lots of Israelite kids grew up in towns and cities. What did *they* do? Well, that depended on what their dad did. Back then boys almost always worked in the family business with their father. They didn't sit around dreaming what they'd be when they grew up. They knew what they'd be doing, and they were already *doing* it. So what kind of jobs did people have back then?

Dung Collector

Remember the guys trampling dung all day to make fertilizer? Well, here's another dirty job: for a fee, a dung collector would go around a city and cart off all the animal dung. Dung was dragged out the Dung Gate in Jerusalem and dumped in the dump. (A guy could get really pooped after a day of this.) Dung collectors also earned money by selling jugs of animal pee to tanners. You're wondering why anyone would buy jugs of donkey pee, right? Read on.

Tanners

A tanner was the guy who turned animal skins into leather. Lots of stuff was made out of leather in Bible days: sandals, pouches, clothing, you name it. For example, the Bible tells us that John the Baptist wore a leather belt, and goatskins were used as wine jugs.

People looked down on tanners because their work was so stinky. You see, to get the fat and grease off the hides, tanners soaked them in animal urine. No telling whose idea *that* was, but the smell was so bad that tanners were ordered to live outside the city. But hey, the apostle Peter stayed with a tanner when he was in Joppa (Acts 9:43).

Fullers

People also looked down on fullers. A fuller was a guy who helped in the process of making cloth by dying or bleaching. A fuller probably also kept big jugs full of pee around his house. Mr. and Mrs. Fuller had to live outside the city too because their house *stunk so badly*! Why? Well, after sheep were sheared, shepherds took the fleeces to the fuller, who degreased and cleaned them by soaking them in pee pots. (This is not where the story of the "golden fleece" began.)

Bleach hadn't been invented yet, so to get cloth really white, fullers stomped it in a mixture of alkali, soap, ashes, sulfur fumes, and putrid urine. (Putrid means it's left to sit in jugs until it gags you.) Later the cloths were trampled clean in water. You would *hope* so!

ABOUT THE FULLERS

If you were born into a fuller family, and your dad couldn't afford to hire workers, chances are everyday you would jog in jugs of pee. Fun! And when you finally did run out to play, think other kids wanted to play with you?

Imagine two high-class ladies walking along: "Jezebel, you simply must tell me! How do you get your robes so white?"

"Well, Hoglah, my fuller uses only the most putrid urine!"

When Mark 9:3 says that Jesus' clothes "became dazzling white, whiter than [any fuller] in the world could bleach them," you know what kind of "bleach" Mark was talking about.

Spinners, Weavers, Dyers

The spinner was next in line. He took the fleece and produced yarn. He used a little hand spindle thingy for this since they didn't have spinning wheels back then.

Afterward, the yarn went to the weaver who wove it into cloth. People looked down on weavers because they thought that weaving wasn't taken seriously as a trade for men. It had been the work of women, who at that time were not the equals of men. Weavers lived in the bad neighborhood, down by the Dung Gate — meaning beside the garbage dump.

After the weavers had made the cloth, dyers took the cloth and dyed it. They got their colors from interesting places. For example, if your robe was crimson, you could be sure it'd been dyed with juice from worms or grubs. Imagine if it was your job to gather worms all day — or to squish them.

Tax Collectors

These guys were hated more than anyone. Even dung collectors, fullers, and tanners looked down on tax collectors. Reason? In the Old Testament times, taxes were sometimes so high that some Jews had to sell their kids as slaves to get money to pay their taxes.

In New Testament times, when the Romans ruled over Israel, they appointed some Jews to collect taxes from the other Jewish people. Some tax collectors were so crooked that they not only made people pay Roman taxes, but cheated them out of *extra* money as well — which they stuffed in their own pockets.

One tax collector named Matthew quit his job to follow Jesus. Another one, Zacchaeus, felt bad about the people he had swindled and paid back all the money back. These two guys were exceptions. Most tax collectors kept on swindling.

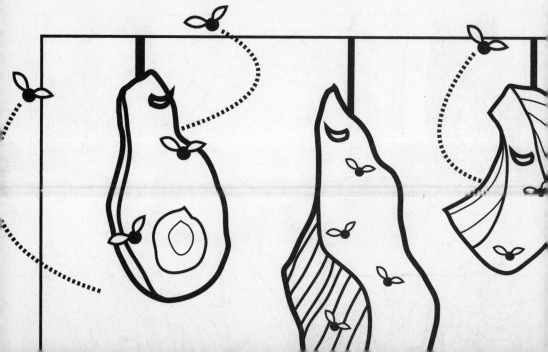

FUN FACT

People didn't eat much meat in ancient Israel, so there weren't many butchers, except in large cities where rich people could afford it. The meat was kosher, meaning all the blood had been drained out of it. But raw meat just hung in the open market until someone bought it. Flies had all the time in the world to crawl all over it and lay eggs in it.

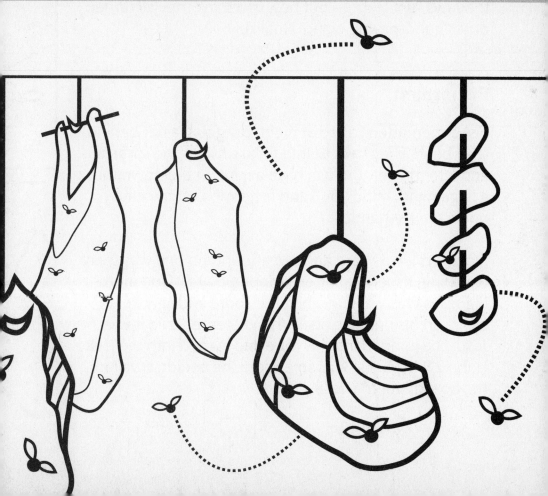

Carpenters

Jesus was a carpenter. If you lived in Nazareth and you needed a door, ox yoke, plow, storage chest, or fancy latticework for your windows, chances are you'd have paid Jesus to make it. Mind you, Jesus was not the only carpenter there. Nazareth was known as a city of carpenters.

Why so many woodworkers? Well, Sepphoris, the capitol of Galilee, was only four miles away, and there was plenty of carpentry work there. Jews weren't supposed to get too close to Gentiles because that made the Jews "unclean" — but hey, you think they all turned down good-paying work? Not likely.

Fishermen

Fishermen often fished at night, dragging a net behind their boat. They held a lamp to lure fish to the surface and into the net. But fish have a mind of their own (not a *large* mind, mind you), and fishermen often came home empty-handed.

Since work was hard and sweaty, and no one was there watching, fisherman often stripped down. One morning Jesus was walking along the shore and saw Peter fishing in his underpants. When Peter realized it was Jesus, he jumped into his robe and leaped into the lake (John 21:4–7). He was so excited, he couldn't wait for the boat to get to shore.

Stable Cleaners

Archaeologists have dug up the horse stables from King Solomon's chariot cities (1 Kings 9:17 – 19). There were hundreds of stables per city. Near the stables were rooms for the grooms who took care of the horses. The grooms fed the horses and brushed them. But imagine if you were the official poop scooper, and it was your job to shovel out all five hundred stables a day!

Other Occupations

There were other jobs in Israel. People were potters, bakers, barbers, engravers, stone masons, gatekeepers, goldsmiths, silversmiths, coppersmiths, judges, lawyers, merchants, musicians, doctors, scribes, sailors, singers, soldiers, household managers, tent makers, etc. But we've covered the grossest ones already.

GET SMARTER

The *good* thing about having to learn the family business back then was that your career choices were easy. If your father was a baker, you were a baker. The *problem* was that you didn't have much choice. And even if you hated baking, you were still a baker. These days you *do* have a choice. So find out what you're good at and like doing; then study hard to make your dream come true.

It can take years of education to get your dream job, so be smart and hold onto it. Don't be like the guy who was the property manager for a rich guy, but was fired because he was dishonest. With his reputation on the line, he only thought he had two career choices left—to become a ditch-digger or a beggar (Luke 16:1–3).

Laws of the Land

The Israelites may have been dirt farmers with dung on their sandals and garlic on their breath, but they had one big thing going for them — God. You see, out of all the nations on earth, God had picked them to be his special people. On their way out of Egypt, they had stopped at Mount Sinai where God gave Moses the Ten Commandments on two stone tablets — and a whole bunch of other laws besides.

Now that they were in the Promised Land, the Israelites were supposed to *obey* God's laws. (What? You thought the stone tablets were just wall decorations?) When they obeyed, God protected them and life was good. When they didn't obey, God sent drought, disease, locust plagues, and invading armies to help them smarten up.

Going to Court

In Israel, if someone committed a crime or broke a law, everyone involved had to come before the priests and the judges. Witnesses testified, and then the judges investigated and considered all the evidence. Judges were under strict orders not to receive bribes from people who wanted a decision in their favor. God told them, "Follow justice and justice alone" (Deuteronomy 16:20).

Roman law courts were more complicated than Israelite courts. But that didn't mean that they were better. Roman lawyers could get away with wild stuff that an Israelite judge would never allow. For example, one time when some Jews took Paul to court in front of an official named Gallio, the chief witness got beat up by a mob, and Gallio didn't even care (Acts 18:12–17).

FUN FACTS

They had prisons in Bible days, but they were not comfortable like prisons today, and they didn't have good food. Prisons were cold, dark cells. Often when people ended up in prison, they were given only bread and water. When Samson was in the Philistine prison, they made him turn a heavy millstone all day to grind grain. But first, they gouged out his eyes and blinded him! Such brutal treatment was common back then.

Rock-hard Law

Parts of the law of Moses were really tough! Obeying the Law was not like a math test where you were doing great if you got 75% on an exam. You had to get 100% or you were cursed. "Cursed is everyone who does not continue to do *everything* written in the Book of the Law." Paul told some opponents in Turkey: "Tell me, you who want to be under the law, are you not *aware* of what the law *says*?" (Galatians 3:10; 4:21).

If someone made an idol or worshiped another god, the whole village was supposed to pick up chunks of rock and batter him until he was dead! Even if it was your brother, or your son or daughter, or your wife or your closest friend, the Law said, "Show him no pity... Your hand must be the first in putting him to death. ... Stone him to death" (Deuteronomy 13:8 – 10).

You could also be stoned for committing adultery, taking the Lord's name in vain, or cursing your father or mother. You could even be executed for working on Saturday. People thought long and hard before breaking the law back then.

Roman Laws

The Romans thought that they were advanced and civilized. They looked down their noses at the Hebrews. Hey, but *their* laws were killers too! If you committed a crime and weren't a Roman citizen, you could be publicly whipped. In fact, when a mob accused Paul and Silas of breaking the law, the judges didn't even give them a trial. They simply ordered them to be beaten with rods (Acts 16:16 – 24).

When Paul accidentally started a riot in Jerusalem, the Roman commander ordered Paul to be flogged. This meant having his back ripped open by the *scourge*, a whip with pieces of bone or metal attached to leather cords. Paul only missed this beating because he informed them that he was a Roman citizen (Acts 22:22 – 29). They weren't allowed to torture Roman citizens — just everybody *else*.

GET DEEPER

With such rock-hard rules, no wonder Paul said that the Israelites were "held *prisoners* by the law, locked up until faith should be revealed" (Galatians 3:23). So what was the point of the rock-hard law of Moses — to turn Israel into one big jail? No. The people needed laws to help them behave and not hurt one another and to lead them to God.

But since it was impossible to keep every rule and regulation, and penalties were so harsh, the Israelites realized that life was more than just endless rule keeping. They needed God's mercy. That's why they were really ready for Jesus when he came along.

Do you want mercy when you blow it? Then show mercy to other kids when they trip up. "Blessed are the merciful, for they will be shown mercy" (Matthew 5:7).

The Levites

When God brought the twelve tribes of
Israel out of Egypt, he made the tribe of Levi
the spiritual workers. The Levites did stuff
like teaching God's Law to the Israelites.
They also took turns working at the Tent of
Meeting — and at the temple when it was built
later. They sacrificed animals, burned incense,
guarded the temple, played music, and sang
to God. They did *not* make Levi blue jeans,
however.

Sacrificing to God

Jesus is the Lamb of God who died on the
cross for our sins (John 1:29). Before Jesus
came, when Israelites sinned, they had to
sacrifice *actual* lambs and goats and bulls to
God. Most people were poor, so it really *cost*
them to kill a lamb. They really *were* sacrificing when they sacrificed a sacrifice. The good
news is, when they sacrificed a lamb at the
Passover Feast, they got to *eat* the lamb. It was
one of the few times they ate meat!

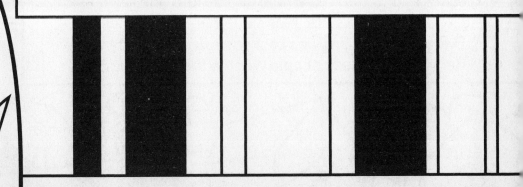

Three Big Feasts

Three times a year all Israelites had to travel to Jerusalem. They had to show up for the Feast of Unleavened Bread (Passover), the Harvest Feast (Pentecost), and the Feast of Ingathering (Exodus 23:14 – 17).

In King David's day, only a couple thousand people called Jerusalem home. By Jesus' day, nearly thirty thousand people lived there. Imagine how crowded it was with a hundred thousand people at feast time! The roads must have been jammed with people. No wonder that one time Joseph and Mary thought Jesus was lost in the crowds (Luke 2:41 – 46).

When the pilgrims first saw Jerusalem from miles away and began ascending up to it, they sang the "Songs of Ascents" — Psalms 120–134. The noise of the singing must have been deafening. It was like a moving music festival!

People with relatives there had a place to stay, and the rich stayed in inns. But where did the *other* pilgrims stay? They camped out around the city. Jews from Galilee descended on the Mount of Olives by the thousands and turned the whole hillside into one huge tent city. Jesus and his disciples slept there sometimes too. Every olive orchard was packed. You really gotta wonder where all these people went to the bathroom.

ENOUGH SACRIFICES!

At times the Israelites were totally disobedient to God, yet they still put on a religious show by sacrificing animals. God said he would rather they were merciful and caring than to do the sacrifice thing (Hosea 6:6).

Can you imagine offering a dead dog to God? Well, Isaiah said that if people didn't love God's Word, that even when they sacrificed a lamb it was like they were killing a dog. If they offered grain, it was like they were giving God pig's blood (Isaiah 66:2–3). Yecch!

God finally got *so* mad at the priests that he said, "I will … spread dung upon your faces, even the dung of your solemn feasts!" (Malachi 2:3, KJV) The New International Version translates dung as offal. This awful offal was the guts and half-digested stomach gook and other yucko stuff from inside an animal. Take your pick: dung or offal.

Sadducees

By Jesus' day, the wealthy priest families and a lot of Levites had morphed into a group called the Sadducees. (That's pronounced *sad*-you-sees.) They were really into ceremonies. Anything to do with the temple or animal sacrifices, they were all over it. Problem was, though they believed in God, they didn't believe in angels or the resurrection from the dead or even in heaven. They *did* believe in gambling on horses though, so when the Romans built a horse-racing stadium in Jerusalem, the Sadducees pulled out their shekels and went on down.

Pharisees

Another group that was big in Jesus' day was the Pharisees. *Pharisees* means "the separate ones," and these guys worked extra hard to be separate from sinners. They weren't into keeping temple rules as much as the Sadducees. They were into living holy lives — *super* holy lives. They loved rules so much they came up with tons of extra rules. Some Pharisees were godly people, but many of them were *self*-righteous.

Teachers of the Law

A scribe's job was to write out copies of the Scriptures. But after spending years writing out verses, they knew the law of Moses inside out. (Try it for a few years. You'll see.) They became such experts that they became top *teachers* of the law. Some scribes were pretty cool guys, but lots of them were hypocrites. Jesus warned, "The teachers of the law . . . do not practice what they preach" (Matthew 23:2–3).

The Common People

When the Pharisees called themselves "the separate ones," they didn't just mean separate from "unclean" Gentiles like most Jews did (Acts 10:28). They wouldn't even associate with *fellow Jews* if they were poor or dirty or not religious enough.

In Jesus' day, poor people were so overtaxed, they struggled just to make it. They didn't have time to keep the Pharisees' endless rules. Some Pharisees would freak if one of these dirty Jews touched them, and they'd rush home to take a bath. Their attitude wold be like the people in Isaiah 65:5 (KJV) who said, "'Stand by thyself,'" they cried, "'come not near to me; for I am holier than thou.'"

But get this: it was these same religious leaders who kept them so poor! Jesus condemned the teachers of

the law for "devour[ing] widows' houses" (Luke 20:47).
They were like religious termites, eating the poor out
of house and home. Jesus loved the poor. He preached
the gospel to them and healed them.

WHITEWASHED TOMBSTONES

In Israel, people were usually buried in caves
or in tombs carved out of the rock. Often whole
families would be buried together in the same
tomb. When they carried a corpse down into
the tomb, there were the other guys—nothing
but bones and ragged burial cloths left. The
mourners quickly left and sealed the stone door
shut tight— *very* tight.

Soon the new body started rotting. John 11:39
says that after four days of being dead, Lazarus
was already stinking. Microbes, like bacteria
and mold, began eating the corpse. Worms
began "feeding sweetly on him" (Job 24:20,
KJV). After a couple weeks, a corpse was
boiling with maggots and germs, and it was an
oozing, stinking mess.

Finally, all the flesh was gone, and only bones
and slime-stained burial cloths were left. And
a *horrible* smell! Jesus said that's what a lot of
the teachers of the Law and the Pharisees were
like: "You are like whitewashed tombs, which
look beautiful on the outside but on the inside
are full of dead men's bones and everything

unclean" (Matthew 23:27). Pretty outside, putrid inside.

The religious leaders said to the poor, "'Keep away; don't come near me for I am too sacred for you!'" (Isaiah 65:5). Jesus turned that around and warned the poor that the religious leaders were like stinky graves that *they* shouldn't touch.

About whitewashing tombs: if someone touched a grave, he was "unclean" for seven days. So to avoid thousands of pilgrims having time-out for a week, the Jews would paint tombs with a fresh coat of white paint just before Passover so that the crowds of pilgrims could see and avoid them.

All in the Family

Ever see a movie where some ruthless guy gets control of a town and gives all the top jobs to his family and friends? That's what happened in Jesus' day. A Sadducee named Annas became the high priest, ruled for years and then got kicked out because he was so corrupt. Did that stop him? Nah.

Annas continued running things from behind the scenes because he got his son Eleazar appointed high priest in his place. When Eleazar's time was up, Annas had his son-in-law, Caiaphas, appointed high priest. After that, Annas's four *other* sons got the top job, one after another. High priests changed, but everyone knew it was old Awful Annas still running things. It was a sad time for a poor man in Israel.

Levite Leather

Why did Annas and sons *want* to control the temple? It was a huge money-making racket, that's why! Remember how tanners took animal skins and made them into leather? Ever wonder where most of those hides *came* from? Well, the priests sacrificed tons of oxen and sheep and goats every day in the temple. After skinning the animals, they sold the hides to tanners. Jerusalem was a major leather-producing city.

FUN FACT

Remember the dung collector? Well, there were also offal collectors. (Offal was another name for animal guts and gloopy insides.) This job really took guts! These gallons of gurgling gook were carted away from the temple to a place outside the city, where they were burned. Imagine packs of dogs going wild when a cartload of guts arrived.

Blood Money

Here is another little-known fact: When animals were slaughtered, all their blood was drained out at the altar. We're talking about *gallons* of blood from every ox! It added up to swimming pools full! What did they *do* with the stuff? The blood drained down an underground channel and filled up a huge pit outside the city walls. Priests then sold the rotting red stuff to gardeners to fertilize the soil. (That is *not* where "blood oranges" come from.)

Sacrificial Lamb Scam

Where Annas and Co. really crossed the line was when they began selling sacrificial animals. The Law said that when Israelites sacrificed an ox or a lamb or a goat, the animal had to be "without defect or blemish" (Leviticus 22:21), meaning they couldn't be sick or have stuff wrong with them. So before anyone sacrificed a lamb, the priests carefully checked it for defects.

Annas's gang would find the teensiest flaw and say, "Sorry, bud. Your lamb doesn't pass inspection. You'll have to buy one of our preapproved specials to sacrifice to God." Yeah, at a high price! And, they kept the animals right in the temple courts! Imagine the noise! Imagine the smell! How could you focus on worshiping God while you were avoiding piles of goat dung and slipping in pools of ox pee?

On top of that, you could only buy sacrificial animals with "holy" Temple shekels — not regular Roman coins — so the moneychangers set up their tables in the temple courtyard too.

GET COOLER

The religious guys were trying to please God by obeying him, but they got into rules so much that they missed the big picture. Remember the story Jesus told about the poor Jewish guy on the road to Jericho? (See Luke 10:25–37.) Robbers mugged him and left him half dead. A priest saw him, but instead of helping, walked on past. Same with a Levite. They were probably in a hurry to get to the temple and worship God.

Only a compassionate Samaritan stopped to help him. The big rule is to love God, but the second big rule is to love your neighbor as you love yourself. That means going out of your way to help others when they need it, like when your kid brother needs help with his homework or your mom needs a hand clearing the table. People don't have to be lying half dead in some ditch to need your help.

Jesus' Daily Life

Jesus wasn't the only religious leader of his day to gather a group of disciples around him and teach them. Lots of rabbis did that. Jesus was a rabbi on the move, though. He didn't stay in one place for long. Jesus usually traveled from village to village, teaching and healing the sick. Sometimes Jesus taught in synagogues, Jewish houses of worship, more often he spoke beside some lake or in an open field.

A Mob of Merry Men and Women

Some people think that Jesus had only twelve disciples. Actually, he had a *huge crowd* of disciples — about 120 people (Acts 1:15). One day, Jesus called together all his disciples, picked twelve of them, and gave those twelve a special name: *apostles* (Luke 6:12 – 16).

Picture a whole mob of men and women following Jesus around, creating their own parade wherever they went. They must have been a sight coming into town! They camped out at night in fields, got the old cook fires going, sat around telling stories, then all bedded down under the stars.

Sometimes Jesus sent most of his disciples out to preach — like when he sent out seventy-two guys at once—and then he would travel light with just the Twelve (Luke 10:1).

FUN FACTS

where did the disciples take showers when they traveled with Jesus? After all, they got sweaty and dirty walking the hot, dusty roads. Well, there weren't any showers, unless they had a major scrub-down at some friend's house. And where did they go poo? Sometimes villagers let them use their toilet, but often they just went beside the road or out behind some sycamore tree.

Women Disciples

You gotta hand it to the women who left their homes and joined Jesus on the dusty roads—Mary Magdalene, Joanna, Susanna, and many others were dedicated disciples. On one trip, even James and John's mom tagged along (Luke 8:1–3; Matthew 20:20).

Ever go out with a bunch of kids and you're dying for a cool drink but no one has cash? Then someone's mom shows up and pays for a "brain freeze" for everyone? Well, Jesus and his disciples were preaching the gospel full-time, so they couldn't hold down jobs. So guess who paid for food and stuff? Women disciples with cash (Luke 8:3).

Many women followed Jesus from Galilee to care for his needs (Matthew 27:55), which meant they were probably lugging water, washing clothes, buying food, cooking, etc. They probably carried cooking pots and spices with them. Can't you just imagine the clinking and clanging of pots as Jesus and his followers walk into a town?

Next time you're tempted to think girls aren't cool, remember this: it was women who kept Jesus on the road.

Eating Wherever

The thing about traveling around Israel was that Jesus and his disciples ate in lots of new places. Some days Jesus and all twelve disciples dined in wealthy Pharisees' homes and sometimes with despised tax collectors. Sometimes God did miracles to provide food for them in a desert. Sometimes they were too busy to even eat. (Can't you hear their stomachs rumbling?) Sometimes they stayed in people's homes and ate whatever they were given. Sometimes when they were traveling, they'd all sit down and eat beside the road.

Under the Stars

Jesus and his disciples often slept in a new place every night with no certain place to lay their heads. Sometimes they slept in the home of rich friends, but more often than not they slept under the trees, on the Mount of Olives, or in somebody's field. Their only blankets were the wool robes they carried around. This was fine in summer, but it wasn't much fun during the rainy season.

Jesus' clothes probably had "the smell of a field" just like Esau's did (Genesis 27:27). They weren't necessarily dirty, but let's put it this way: when Jesus was transfigured on a mountain and "his clothes became as white as the light" (Matthew 17:2), well, that was the cleanest they'd ever looked.

It was a good thing some helpers tagged along sometimes to do the laundry. Otherwise the twelve apostles would've been called the Dirty Dozen.

WHAT'S IN IT FOR ME?

Jesus' disciples were convinced that he was the Messiah who would set up the kingdom of Israel—right then and there. In fact, Jesus promised them that they would sit on twelve thrones with him, judging the twelve tribes of Israel. Thrones? Cool! So cool, in fact, that the apostles never got it out of their minds. James and John tried to push to the head of the line and get the thrones on Jesus' left and right hand. That got the other ten apostles steamed.

Cleaning Out the Temple

Remember how Annas and sons turned the temple courts into a market? When Jesus first began preaching and came to Jerusalem, he made a whip out of cords and whipped the cattle and sheep out of there. He threw over the moneychangers' tables and shouted at the dove merchants, "Get these *out* of here! How dare you turn my Father's house into a market!" (John 2: 16).

Three years later, Jesus rode into Jerusalem, entered the temple and — surprise, surprise — there they were again! *Again* Jesus kicked over the money tables and drove the merchants out. "My house will be called a house of prayer," he bellowed, "but you are making it a den of robbers!" (Matthew 21:13). This time Jesus didn't warn the dove sellers. He just kicked over *their* benches too.

Jesus shut the whole place down and wouldn't let any-one carry merchandise though the temple courts. The courts were about the size of an acre, so Jesus had to shout pretty loud every time a merchant tried to sneak across a far court.

Jesus put a dent in the priests' profits and scared them so much that they wanted him dead. They paid one of Jesus' disciples, Judas, to betray him. They arrested Jesus and took him to the Roman governor, Pilate, to have him crucified.

GET STRONGER

Jesus' first disciples didn't have a lot of comforts that we enjoy today. They didn't have fridges, 20-inch TVs, video games, air conditioners, stereo systems, soft beds, showers, or clean bathrooms. Back then, if you followed Jesus around, you were truly roughin' it. Guess what? Millions of Christians today, in countries like India and China, live in conditions very similar to how Jesus and his disciples lived.

You may not be facing real hardships right now, but life can be hard in a lot of different ways when you're following Jesus. Make up your mind right now that you will stand strong no matter what happens. Paul gave this invitation two thousand years ago: "Endure hardship with us like a good soldier of Christ Jesus" (2 Timothy 2:3). It still applies today.

Falling off the Roof

Since house roofs in Israel were flat, people walked around on them. Problem was, you could fall off while admiring the view. That was why the law said that you had to build a *parapet*, a low wall, around your rooftop. That didn't stop some guys from doing dangerous stuff. Since roofs were flat and houses were close together, people would jump from roof to roof. They did it *so much* that rabbis called it "the road of the roofs." Well, sometimes you *had* to escape without going down into your house (Matthew 24:17).

Flying Ax-heads

The Bible talks several times about ax heads flying off the handle. It was enough to make a guy not want to chop wood. One day some prophets were chopping down trees, and this guy took a good old swing and — *Whoosh!* — the ax-head went sailing. Fortunately it landed in the water instead of another prophet. Other times though, ax heads would go shooting out, hit other woodcutters, and kill them (Deuteronomy 19:5; 2 Kings 6:5).

Gored by Cattle

In Bible days, every village had oxen. Back then they had long, deadly horns. Some of them had a mean temper and would gore people. Worse yet, oxen weren't always tied up. In cattle country like Bashan, cattle were turned loose part of the year to find pasture, and some of them got to be pretty wild — especially when they were hungry.

Lion Season

For thousands of years, wild animals like lions lived down in the lush forests along the Jordan River. Problem was, every spring the rains and melting snow made the Jordan overflow its banks. Wet, hungry lions escaped the floods and ended up walking around Israelite neighborhoods looking for something — or some*one* — to eat.

Dying in Battle

If you read the Old Testament, you'll notice how *many* men die in a single battle! When King Abijah of Judah and his soldiers fought Israel's soldiers, "Abijah and his men inflicted heavy losses on them, so that there were five hundred thousand casualties among Israel's able men" (2 Chronicles 13:17). Half a million dead? Yeah, that *was* heavy losses all right! Sword fighting was brutal. Spend all day fighting a mob of men trying to kill you, and sooner or later you get tired and some guy gets you.

NOT-SO-FUN FACT

Back then when some guy died, his family not only wept and mourned, but they also ripped their clothes, put dirt on their heads, and rolled around in ashes. What was really strange was how wealthy families often hired professional mourners to help mourn. These men and women didn't even know the guy who'd died, but were paid to cry and wail loudly. They also beat their breasts and pulled out their hair — although that was probably more expensive.

PUS AND PAIN

Even if you didn't get killed right in the battle, you could end up with incurable wounds from arrows in your back and liver. Result? You'd die a few days after the battle. Another thing, wounds *often* became infected and festered. *Festering* is when a wound has lots of pus and becomes disgusting and stinky. In Bible times they didn't have antibiotics, so more soldiers may have died from infected wounds than died in the battle.

Intestines Spilling Out

After Judas betrayed Jesus, he realized what a horrible thing he'd one, but it was too late. Judas hurled the money on the temple floor and left. He ran across the city and out the Dung Gate toward the city dump. The gospel of Matthew says Judas hung himself, but the book of Acts says he fell and his intestines spilled out. So if we put all this information together, here's what might have happened:

Judas probably looked for something to kill himself with. He found an old piece of rope and decided to hang himself. Olive trees grew on the steep hill overlooking the dump, so Judas tied a noose around his neck, threw the other end over a branch, tied it, and then jumped. The rotten rope broke, Judas fell and hit a sharp rock, and his guts burst open. As he rolled down toward the garbage dump, all his intestines came spilling out. Blood was everywhere. It was such a gruesome sight that people called that place the Field of Blood (Matthew 27:1 – 8; Acts 1:18 – 19).

Crucifixion

Meanwhile, Jesus' religious enemies took him to the Romans who ordered him to be whipped with a cat-o'-nine-tails. His back and arms and legs were ripped open by the metal on the end of the whips until he was bleeding everywhere. If you've seen the movie *The Passion of the Christ*, you know this was serious stuff! Then they took him out to be crucified.

The Romans only executed slaves and "undesirables" this way. Crucifixion was not only a painful death, but was very humiliating: crosses were set up in public places where people passing by could see the person hanging there. This is how Jesus died.

First, nails were driven through Jesus' wrists and feet. This was painful enough, but then when the cross was then set up, he was hanging from the nails and couldn't breathe. He had to pull himself up with his arms just to take a breath. When he got tired, he'd slump down again and hang there. When he needed more air, he had to pull himself up again. After hours of this, he got so tired he could barely pull himself up anymore.

On top of it, all that body weight hanging there pulled a man's arms out of joint. The pain was incredible. Often the Roman soldiers didn't give the condemned man anything to drink, so he went crazy with thirst. This slow, painful death sometimes lasted days. The reason Jesus died after only six hours on the cross may have been because he had lost so much blood from being whipped.

Get Deeper

Jesus knew ahead of time that he would suffer a horrible beating and then be crucified. He knew it. So why didn't he run away? Why didn't he let his disciples fight to protect him? They were ready. Jesus could have gotten out of it if he'd really wanted to.

Jesus chose to die because he knew that was the only way to pay the full price for your sins. All the sacrificial lambs and bulls and goats just weren't cutting it. They covered a one-time sin, but people were back again a short time later, needing to do it all over again. Jesus was the perfect Lamb of God who could once and for all and forever take away your sins.

Jesus died for you because he loved you. He loved you that much. Will you accept his free gift of forgiveness and eternal life?

Luke 2:52

Bible FReaks & geeks

written by Ed Strauss
illustrated by Erwin Haya

kidz

FUN FACT

Many English slang words come from other languages like French, German, Icelandic, and Italian. In fact, our word slang probably began as a Norwegian word. In parts of Norway, slang means offensive language. When guys stood around calling each other names, their argument used to be called a slanging match.

Dog Names

Job and his pals weren't the only slang slingers. The Israelites had some real zingers. One day a king named Ish-Bosheth accused his top general, Abner, of being disloyal. Abner shouted back, "Am I a dog's head?" (2 Samuel 3:8). *Dog's head* meant a worthless traitor. You gotta wonder who came up with that term.

Once King David and his men were fleeing for their lives and a guy named Shimei stood by the road screaming, "Get out, get out, you man of blood, you scoundrel!" (2 Samuel 16:7). (A *scoundrel* is a lowlife.)

This ticked off David's cousin Abishai. "Why should this dead dog curse my lord the king?" he asked. "Let me go over and cut off his head" (2 Samuel 16:9). *Dead dog* was a slang expression that meant that Shimei was dead meat. Fortunately for Shimmy, David told his cousin to just keep on walking.

New Testament Slang

The Jews called Gentiles dogs, but *dog* also meant *any* dude doing bad stuff. The apostle Paul warned, "Watch out for those dogs, those men who do evil" (Philippians 3:2). You didn't want to be called a dog back then. Dogs didn't make it to heaven (Revelation 22:12–15).

Then there's *fox*. Once some guys warned Jesus to get out of King Herod's territory. They said, "Leave this place and go somewhere else. Herod wants to kill you." Jesus replied, "Go tell that fox, 'I must keep going'" (Luke 13:31–33). A fox is cunning, but that's not only what Jesus was getting at. Herod is not just a man of words, but of action—fox-like action.

OUTGROWING LABELS

Be careful not to brand some kid with a label like loser or imbecile just because he acts dumb now. People change. Case in point: one night the prophet Daniel had a vision of a ferocious lion with wings. Suddenly its wings were torn off—Ouch! That had to hurt!—and God stood Leo up on two feet like a man, plucked out his beast heart, and replaced it with a kind human heart (Daniel 7:2-4).

This vision wasn't about some lion angel. It was about Nebuchadnezzar, king of Babylon. Neb started off as a proud, power-hungry bully, but God humbled him and he changed into a good guy who loved God.

The point being, even bad dudes can change. If you're a Christian, you're a work in progress, meaning that God hasn't given up on you and you'll grow up. So hold out hope for other kids too.

GET COOLER

When you're mad, you're most tempted to sling slang. Maybe you don't clench your fists, turn red in the face, and start screaming insults, so you don't think you have a problem with anger. But if you call people hurtful names when they bug you, you have issues.

The solution is to ditch anger. Can it be done? Yes it can. Proverbs 29:11 says, "A fool gives full vent to his anger, but a wise man keeps himself under control." How does a wise man do that? How can *you* keep yourself under control?

King David had a solution. He said, "I will put a muzzle on my mouth as long as the wicked are in my presence" (Psalm 39:1). What? Like a *doggie muzzle*? Yup. You got the picture—like a dog muzzle—only this is a parable. David meant that he was gonna bite his tongue. Try it next time you're tempted to call someone names.

Bible Freaks & Geeks
Written by Ed Strauss

Softcover • ISBN 0-310-71309-9

Boys today—Christian kids included—constantly label each other, and do it almost without thinking. This book explores the meanings behind these names and gives humorous examples from the Bible that either explains their accuracy or disproves them as stereotypes.